NATO

PETER L. FERRARA

NATO
AN ENTANGLED ALLIANCE

A GROLIER COMPANY

Franklin Watts
New York | London | Toronto | Sydney | 1984
An Impact Book

Map courtesy of Vantage Art, Inc.

Photographs courtesy of:
UPI: pp. 6, 19, 33, 46, 57, 64, 71, 79;
AP/Wide World: pp. 23, 30.

Library of Congress Cataloging in Publication Data

Ferrara, Peter L.
NATO, an entangled alliance.

(An Impact book)
Bibliography: p.
Includes index.
Summary: Explores such critical issues as the changing
economic status of the United States and Western Europe,
the global role of NATO, the different views of détente
and the Soviet threat held by Americans and Europeans,
and the possible future of the NATO alliance.
1. North Atlantic Treaty Organization—Juvenile
literature. [1. North Atlantic Treaty Organization]
I. Title. II. Title: N.A.T.O., an entangled alliance.
UA646.3.F47 1984   355'.031'091821   84-10399
ISBN 0-531-04759-8

CONTENTS

INTRODUCTION

For over three decades, NATO—the North Atlantic Treaty Organization—has provided Western Europe and its other member nations with a framework for security and a common defense, safeguarding its members from any potential military aggression. In the past ten years, however, this network for Western security has become a deeply troubled alliance. Minor disagreements and even short-term crises have beset the Atlantic Alliance (as it's also called) since its very beginning in 1949. Since the 1970s, however, numerous important issues have created serious and long-lasting rifts between key alliance members, particularly between the United States and various West European nations.

The present problems which divide the NATO alliance occur at an especially bad time—a time when an unprecedented number of challenges all across the globe threaten Western security. The conflict between the superpowers—between East and West—has become wider and more acute in the past decade, throughout previously untroubled regions of the world and in Europe, too. Regional conflicts in Africa, the Middle East, in Central America, and in the Caribbean are also enmeshed in wider American and Soviet competition. In light of these growing challenges to Western security and unity, NATO's increasing inability to either act or speak in a united voice on several key issues has cast serious doubt on its effectiveness as an allied defense system, on its role in global events, and on its economic and political solidarity. Many foreign affairs critics believe that NATO worked as a strategy for military security in the postwar 1940s and 1950s but is simply inadequate for the more complex problems of the 1980s, given the economic and military changes that have occurred over the past thirty-five years.

Two views predominate. One view maintains that the present troubles of NATO are similar to the problems that have always plagued the organization, and they will be resolved as they always have been in the past. Another less optimistic view declares that the present problems are fundamentally different in nature than the early NATO disputes and reflect deep and divergent policy differences that cannot and will not be resolved.

This book will explore some critical issues. These include the changing economic status of the United States and Western Europe, the global role of NATO, the different views of détente and the Soviet threat held by Americans on one hand and Europeans on the other, and the problems created by "strategic parity," a concept that is examined in detail in a separate chapter. The various views regarding the future of the NATO alliance and the prospects for NATO's successful adaptation to the new challenges which it faces today will also be examined.

CHAPTER ONE

PRELUDE
TO
NATO

orld War II raged across the European continent and North Africa from 1939 to 1945. The United States, Great Britain, and the Soviet Union (the Big Three), and such other nations as Canada, Australia, New Zealand, and France (the Free French only) fought as allies against Nazi Germany, Japan, Italy, and other "axis" countries. At the war's end, after the smoke of six years of bitter battles had lifted, all of Europe was literally shattered. Most major European cities either had been bombed or had been the sites of fierce combat; the once-pastoral European countryside was torn apart and littered with artillery and bomb craters and the rubble and debris of armored battles.

The armies of all European nations, except that of Great Britain, had been quickly and thoroughly decimated by the lightning attacks of the German forces. In September of 1939, German forces invaded Poland; in 1940, they swept north through Norway and Denmark and then down through the Netherlands and Belgium. By June of 1940, the Germans had easily defeated the French, marched into Paris, and forced the British troops in France to make an emergency evacuation across the English Channel. The Germans were in control of all of Europe west of Poland, except Great Britain which, situated across the English Channel remained free of Nazi German occupation forces. The Germans were never able to launch a successful invasion against Great Britain, due in large part to the Royal Air Force which won the battles for the skies above Great Britain. Millions of soldiers and civilians on both sides died during the course of the war.

Equally as devastated at the war's end were the once-thriving economies of the European nations. The industrial plants, the agricultural lands, and the power stations were almost completely destroyed across the continent. The Soviet Union was likewise ruined economically by the war; only the economy of the United States emerged strong and healthy from the war. Throughout the war the United States extended massive economic and military material support to Great Britain and the Soviet Union through the "lend-lease" program. Billions of dollars worth of arms and goods were shipped across the North Atlantic to England and to the Soviets' Arctic port of Murmansk. Friendly relations and cooperation between the United States and the Soviet Union reached its pinnacle during the war, symbolized by the famous photograph of American and Soviet soldiers reaching to shake hands across a shattered bridge on the Elbe River in Germany in April 1945 as the two armies were linked.

MISTRUST AMONG ALLIES

Despite the relationship between the Big Three as allies, a deep vein of mistrust developed during the latter years of the war. Various factors contributed to this climate of East-West mistrust. Not only was there a general dislike of each other's postwar intentions and ambitions, there were also confusing foreign policy signals being sent by the Soviets and by the Americans and British. In 1939, the Soviet Union had signed a nonaggression pact with Nazi Germany, in the futile hopes of avoiding a war. The pact, which was nullified by the German attack on the Soviet Union in 1941, divided Poland between Germany and the Soviet Union. After signing the nonaggression pact in 1939, the Soviets attacked, without any provocation, the small democratic state of Finland and annexed a large portion of its port territory on the northerly Barents Sea. On the western side of the coin, the United States in 1943 after bombing Rome reached a secret surrender agreement with a group of Fascists who had overthrown Mussolini, the Italian dictator. In essence, the agreement guaranteed that the

Allies in World War II, American and Soviet
soldiers link up on the Elbe River near
Torgau, Germany, on April 25, 1945.

Italian army would be neutral for the rest of the war and in return the same political group and people who ran Italy before and during the war would be allowed to remain in power. It was a bad agreement which increased Soviet suspicions, but it was calculated to save American lives.

Another major episode which bred mistrust between the Soviets and the Americans and British was the delay in opening a second, west European front against the Germans. The Soviets who had fought the bulk of the German armies for almost three years, mostly on native soil, had asked their American and British allies to open up a second front in western Europe to relieve some of the German pressure on the Soviet Red Army. The German invasion pushed deep into the Soviet heartland, occupying some of its prime industrial and agricultural lands, and coming literally to the gates of Moscow. The invasion was taking a devastating toll on the Soviets, in the destruction of factories, equipment, and lives—estimated at some 20 million civilians and soldiers. The United States and Great Britain agreed to open a second front, but a lack of American military preparedness forced a long delay. Until the Japanese attack on Pearl Harbor at the end of 1941, the political climate in the United States prevented full war mobilization, and in 1941 there were still only 1.6 million soldiers in the American armed forces. In 1942, a joint American-British force invaded North Africa, and in 1943, Italy. By 1944, American forces had completely driven German forces out of Italy, and in 1944, the major, second front so desperately needed by the Soviets was created with the Allied D-day landing on the beaches of Normandy in northern France. Soon thereafter the Soviets began to push the German army back across eastern Europe while American, British, Canadian, Dutch, and Free French forces tightened the circle by driving the Germans eastward.

Stalin, the Soviet dictator, mistrusted American and British motives and suspected that the delay in opening a second front was intentional, based on Anglo-American intentions to control large areas of Europe after the war. Stalin even thought that the British and Americans were engaged in secret surrender agreements with the Germans. The front was not opened sooner, however, because there were insufficient troops and supplies for an early, successful invasion of western Europe by an Anglo-American force.

Similar confusions which bred further mistrust surrounded the battle for Berlin in 1945. In April, American and Soviet forces were equidistant from Berlin, coming from the east and the west. General Eisenhower, the Supreme Allied Commander, reportedly believed that allowing the Soviets to capture Berlin, the capital of Nazi Germany, would convince the Soviets of the West's goodwill since it would be a great honor for a victorious army. He also thought that Berlin was militarily insignificant. Winston Churchill, the British Prime Minister, disagreed and argued for a quick Anglo-American assault on Berlin. President Roosevelt overruled the dispute, and the Soviets were allowed to enter and take the city. The Soviet Red Army did capture Berlin after a fierce battle which took over 100,000 Soviet lives, and Germany surrendered on May 7, 1945, ending the war in Europe.

TERRITORIAL AMBITIONS

The single most crucial issue which divided the Allies and transformed them into rivals was who would control the territories occupied by the Allied forces. If there was confusion about postwar territorial claims, Soviet ambitions became clear to the United States and Great Britain at the Yalta Conference held by the Big Three in early 1945. At Yalta, Germany was divided into four zones to be occupied by the British, the Americans, the French, and the Soviets. Berlin, which was deep in the Soviet zone, was divided in a similar manner into four sectors, each governed by the local military commander. Stalin declared at Yalta that "whoever occupies a territory also imposes on it his own social system." Stalin's declaration meant that the Soviet Union would establish "friendly" governments in the East European countries. In practice, this meant that Communist governments, marked by an absence of the basic freedoms of speech, assembly, religion, elections, and enterprise which were so dear to the West, would be set up in all Soviet-occupied territories. At the war's end, the Soviet Union occupied all of Eastern Europe.

The postwar conflict between the two superpowers which led directly to the formation of the NATO alliance was focused on the destiny of two nations—Germany and Poland. In 1940, a Polish government-in-exile had been set up in London. In late 1945, as the Soviets pushed back the Germans, Stalin established an alternative government in the Soviet-occupied city of Lublin, southeast of Warsaw. The Lublin government as it was known was composed of Polish Communists from that city. In 1945, when the Soviets had completely occupied Poland, Stalin recognized the Lublin group as the official government of Poland. Churchill and Roosevelt insisted on free elections in Poland, which would include the London-based Poles. Instead, Stalin tightened his grip on Poland, suppressing all elections and all other basic freedoms. In early 1945, Roosevelt tried to use American economic power to force Soviet cooperation on the issue of elections in Poland. In 1945, the American economy was booming and the Soviets, whose economy was shattered, still depended on American lend-lease economic aid. The West, however, was unwilling to accept the Soviet domination of Eastern Europe, and Roosevelt stopped all shipments of goods to the Soviet Union and repeatedly turned down Soviet requests for loans of $5 billion and then $1 billion.

Why was Poland so important an issue? It was important because it is at the crossroads of Eastern and Western

Europe, and it was the traditional invasion corridor into the Soviet Union which the Germans had crossed twice in thirty years. For the West, it also formed a buffer zone against potential attacks in the future by Soviet forces. In any case, not only did Stalin tighten his hold on Poland but proceeded to do the same throughout Eastern Europe.

The postwar status of Germany was another, and perhaps the key, factor that ignited the superpower rivalry in Europe and led to the birth of NATO. The United States and Great Britain were interested in the reunification of Germany. They wanted a demilitarized, self-sufficient, industrial Germany which would add to the strength of Western Europe. The Soviets and the French wanted a weak and divided Germany.

At the Yalta Conference it was not only agreed to divide Germany into occupation zones; it was also agreed that Germany would pay $20 billion in war reparations, with half going to the Soviet Union. Moreover, since the Ruhr, Germany's prime industrial area was in the British zone of occupation, and the prime agricultural lands were in the Soviet zone, an exchange of industrial equipment for food would occur between the two zones.

After Yalta, the Soviets began to dismantle and strip their occupation zone of its limited industrial factories and send them back to the Soviet Union. After the German surrender, they also began using highly skilled German workers to manufacture goods in their zone for shipment back home. In retaliation, in mid-1946, the United States halted all reparations payments being made from the Western zones to the Soviet Union.

Establishing the boundaries of postwar Europe and creating a peace treaty with Germany were the goals of the American, British, and Soviet leaders at the Potsdam (Germany) Conference in July 1945. The results of the conference were that Germany was divided, with the Soviets controlling approximately one-third of the country and the United States, Great Britain, and France the remainder of the nation. "Spheres of influence" over European countries were also acknowledged by the Big Three. The Soviet Union dominated all of East Europe, and annexed Estonia, Latvia, Lithuania, and part of Finland. Yugoslavia, Czechoslovakia, and Albania were given a more independent status by the Soviets.

In 1946, the Soviets attempted to expand their sphere of influence in Iran, Turkey, and later in Greece, although it had been recognized at Potsdam that Greece and the Middle East were of particular interest to the British. Soviet tanks were sent to their country's border with Iran, and Soviet troops which were supposed to be withdrawn from Iran in accord with an earlier agreement between the Big Three would not leave the country. The Soviets wanted a share in Iran's oil concessions which were held by British and American, as well as Iranian, companies. President Truman threatened to use military force to expel the Soviets, a threat that was given additional impact by the recent explosion of the first atomic bomb. The Soviets ordered their troops out of the country. Next, the Soviets tried to pressure another neighbor, Turkey, into joint control of the Dardanelles Straits which command the Soviet navy's passage from the Black Sea into the Mediterranean. An American naval fleet was sent into the Straits, and the Soviet demands were dropped. In Greece, free elections were held in 1946 under British supervision, and a pro-Western political party won. Immediately after the British pulled out of Greece in early 1947, due to their own economic problems, Greek Communists supported with arms and supplies from the Soviet-bloc states of Bulgaria and Yugoslavia began a civil war. The United States sent $400 million in military and economic aid, which eventually led to the defeat of the Communists.

The picture of Europe immediately following the war was a bleak portrait of a continent divided into free states in the West and communist states in the East. The actions of the Soviets in both establishing itself as the totally dominant power in Eastern Europe and in attempting to expand its influence into neighboring countries in areas outside of Europe (Iran, Turkey) provided the background for and pointed to the need for the formation of an alliance of the Western powers. Winston Churchill, in a famous speech given at Fulton, Missouri on March 5, 1946 with President Truman at his side, neatly summarized Soviet actions in Europe and the Middle East by declaring that

> From Stettin in the Baltic to Trieste in the Adriatic, an iron curtain has descended across the continent. Behind that line . . . all are subject in one form or another, not only to Soviet influence but to a very high and increasing measure of control from Moscow.

Churchill went on to state that the Soviet Union wanted "the indefinite expansion of their power and doctrines," and he called for a "fraternal association of English-speaking peoples" to oppose Soviet expansionism.

A Soviet-occupied Poland and East Germany made, in the Western view, all of Western Europe highly vulnerable to a potential Soviet attack. Reinforcing this fear was the fact that in one year the United States Army, which had begun demobilization, was reduced from a force of 8 million soldiers to 1 million and the United States Navy from 3.5 million to less than 1 million. The Soviet Red Army, which remained at near wartime strength of 4 million soldiers, represented by far the largest fighting force on the European continent. Something had to be done to defend Western Europe from potential Soviet expansion.

CHAPTER TWO

THE BIRTH OF NATO

CZECH COUP, BERLIN BLOCKADE, AND

THE FAILURE OF THE UNITED NATIONS

The outlook for Western Europe in 1947 was grim. Europe was weak and defenseless; its economies were ruined. The United States and the Soviet Union emerged from the war as the world's two major superpowers, but within a year after the war's end American troops, as a result of pressure to "bring the boys home," had completely demobilized. The Soviet Red Army, which remained at near wartime levels, outnumbered American troops in Europe by a ten to one margin. The Soviets who had completely occupied and dominated Eastern Europe had also begun to stir up trouble outside of their sphere of influence in Turkey (1946), Iran (1946), and Greece (1947).

Sparked by the events in Turkey, Iran, and Greece, President Truman, who believed that the Soviets were bent on world domination, expressed a new determination to meet the Soviet challenge in his March 1947 speech to Congress. In what was to become known as the Truman Doctrine or the policy of "containment," he declared that the policy of the United States was "to support free peoples who are resisting attempted subjugation by armed minorities or by outside pressures." Containment, which would shape American foreign policy for nearly thirty years, would also include, in the words of Soviet foreign policy expert George Kennan, "the vigilant application of counter-force at a series of constantly shifting geographical points, corresponding to the shifts and maneuvers of Soviet policy." This policy was designed to "contain" Soviet influence wherever it surfaced in the world. The $400 million economic and military aid granted to Greece in 1947 was one of the earliest "applications" of the Truman Doctrine. Over the next three decades further applications of the containment policy would occur in Malaysia, Korea, and Vietnam, and would create grave internal differences among the NATO allies.

The Soviets tightened their grip on their satellite states, and it was clear that no elections were to be held in Poland, in Rumania, in Bulgaria, or anywhere in Eastern Europe. In August of 1947, the Soviets cracked down on all political opposition to communism in Hungary. The cold war between the United States and the Soviet Union began over the issue of the control of Eastern Europe.

At the end of World War II, the United States was the only nation with the economic resources to resolve the postwar restoration and reconstruction problems in Europe. In 1947, after having visited Europe, George Marshall, the Secretary of State, recognized the seriousness of the total economic devastation in Western Europe and its inability to recover quickly. Marshall realized that the only true way for Europe to defend itself against possible attack from the Soviets was to build healthy, strong economies so that European states could field and support their own troops. His plan, which provided for the economic restoration of Europe, became known as the Marshall Plan (1947). The plan called for pumping vast sums of money ($4 billion in four years and $17 billion overall) into Europe and, more importantly, for including Germany in the restoration process. Cleverly, the plan also acted as an arm of the containment policy since it aimed to unify Europe by requiring that the European nations submit a common integrated plan for aid to the United States.

The plan offered wide-scale free economic aid but would grant it only on the basis of joint Europe-wide requests, not on a single-nation basis. This prompted Europeans to create such common organizations as the European Coal and Steel Community. The Marshall Plan aimed to save Europe from chaos, open up trade relations with the United States, prevent such nations as France and Italy (which were nearly bankrupt) from falling to the communists, and stimulate general economic growth. The United States also invited the Soviets to participate in the recovery program, on the condition that the East European economies be integrated with those of Western Europe. The Soviets feared both the economic influences of Western democracies in Eastern Europe and the creation of a strong Western economic bloc.

The Soviets proposed that each European nation pursue a separate reconstruction course, but were turned down by the British, French, and the other European nations. The Soviets then withdrew their participation from the proposed Marshall Plan and began their own recovery program. Poland and Czechoslovakia wanted to join the Plan, but the Soviets would not allow them to participate. In effect, the Marshall Plan united postwar Europe.

Several events in the late 1940s hastened the birth of the NATO alliance. In February 1948 there was a Soviet-backed Communist coup in Czechoslovakia where the pro-Western President and the Communist Prime Minister had come to power two years earlier in free elections. One of the leading pro-Western government officials was assassinated, and the Communists took complete control of the government. Toward the end of World War II, the Allies made plans to establish an organization that would keep peace throughout the world after the war. In 1945, the United Nations was established in San Francisco with fifty-one participating members. The new organization was to provide the postwar world with a means of avoiding wars through consultation and debate, and if necessary, approved U.N. military intervention. All peacekeeping actions were, and are, controlled by the Security Council, composed of five permanent nations—the United States, the Soviet Union, Great Britain, China, and France—and ten elected, temporary members. In matters of grave concern, in crises, any of the Security Council can veto or officially reject a resolution to intervene in or condemn a conflict. When the Soviet supported coup in Czechoslovakia was put before the Security Council in February 1948, a resolution to condemn the coup and perhaps to intervene was vetoed by the Soviet Union. The veto power of one of the five permanent members of the Security Council quickly illustrated the ineffectiveness of the United Nations as a genuine peacekeeping organization. This early failure of the United Nations bred new fears in Europe and on March 17, 1948, France, Great Britain, Belgium, and Luxembourg signed the Brussels Treaty, a mutual defense agreement.

The struggle to bring Germany back into the European community as an independent, strong industrial state, and to maintain control over the western sectors of Berlin were two other conflicts which led to the founding of NATO. During the two years following the war, it became clear that terms of a peace treaty with Germany that would be acceptable to all four countries occupying the country were not attainable. Furthermore, the Soviets and the French did not want a reunified Germany, whereas the United States did. After Stalin's fist had come down on Eastern Europe, especially in Poland, Czechoslovakia, and Hungary, Truman and his policy advisors realized that Germany—which was in the heart of Europe, at the gateway of East and West between the Soviet Union and Western Europe, and had highly productive steel mills and coal mines—must be pro-Western and independent. To this end, the three Western powers decided in the summer of 1948 to join together all three of their occupation zones into a single West German state. There was also much public discussion in the West of rearming the new state of West Germany; it was evident to American military planners that the only way to have sufficient troops to defend Western Europe would be to get them from the West European nations themselves, of which West Germany was the largest. European countries that had been invaded by Germans a few years earlier rejected this suggestion. Instead of quickly rearming Germany, it was decided that a Western defense organization which could be linked to the signers of the Brussels Treaty would be formed.

The problems in the divided city of Berlin, which was deep in the Soviet zone, also finally reached a crisis point. In June 1948, the three Western powers put into use a currency that was good in all Western sectors and announced intentions to unify the three sectors as had been done in West Germany. The Soviet response was swift. In late June 1948, they cut off all electricity, coal, and other supplies to the Western sectors and put an overall blockade on West Berlin. Surrounded by Soviet-dominated territory, Berlin was effectively cut off from its Western allies. A few days later however, the American military commander of Berlin, General Clay, began a twenty-four-hour airlift of supplies to the city. Eventually, in February 1949, after 323 days, the Soviet blockade was broken, and regular supply lines to the city were reestablished. The airlift, and the Berlin Crisis, as it was called, became a symbol of freedom throughout the world. It demonstrated Western resolve to hold onto Berlin and, perhaps more importantly, American ability and commitment to defend Europe against Soviet dreams of domination. Berlin was divided into East and West Berlin.

The Soviet blockade also fueled already-existing European fears about Soviet policy and brought the sense of an immediate Soviet military threat into focus. Shortly after the Brussels Treaty was signed, France and Belgium asked Secretary of State Marshall to work on plans for a common European defense system which would include the involvement of the United States and other European states. Details of the common defense system were worked out over the following year. In Washington, D.C. on April

American soldiers prepare to unload milk for the people of West Berlin during the 1948 blockade.

4, 1949, representatives of Belgium, Canada, Denmark, France, Great Britain, Iceland, Italy, Luxembourg, the Netherlands, Norway, Portugal, and the United States signed the North Atlantic Treaty. The original twelve members eventually grew to sixteen as Greece and Turkey joined in 1952, West Germany in 1955, and Spain in 1982. Three of the most important of the Treaty's fourteen articles are as follows:

> Article 5: The parties agree that an armed attack against one or more of them in Europe or North America shall be considered an attack against them all, and consequently agree that, if such an armed attack occurs, each of them . . . will assist the party or parties so attacked by taking forthwith, individually and in concert with the other parties, such action as it deems necessary, including the use of armed force, to restore and maintain the security of the North Atlantic area . . .

> Article 6: For the purpose of Art. 5 an armed attack on one or more of the parties is deemed to include an armed attack on the territory of any of them in Europe or North America, on the Algerian Departments of France, on the Occupation forces of any party in Europe . . .

> Article 9: The parties hereby establish a Council, on which each of them shall be represented, to consider matters concerning the implementation of the treaty. The Council shall be so organized as to be able to meet promptly at any time. It shall set up such subsidiary bodies as may be necessary . . .

Article 5 provided for actual defense, and Article 6 addressed a complex issue which would create problems time after time over the following decades—the common defense of overseas territories of the NATO members.

Article 9 authorized the permanent military command and planning groups of the North Atlantic Treaty Organization. Events rushed forward in 1949. In May, the Soviets lifted the blockade of Berlin. The West German state came into existence on May 23, 1949, and the NATO pact was ratified by the U.S. Senate and signed by President Truman on July 23, 1949.

NATO was, according to the letter of the defense agreement, a treaty among equals but from the outset depended on the automatic military involvement of the United States in response to any attack on its members. And the American military guarantee consisted of the threat to use atomic bombs in the event of an attack because the small number of conventional ground forces in Western Europe would be unable to repel any sizeable invasion. The implications of the phrases, "among equals" and "the American military guarantee" would grow increasingly complex and difficult over the following thirty-five years of the alliance.

NATO was the crowning achievement of Truman's policy of containment. But it had deep roots in a long tradition of cooperation among the American, British, Canadian, and French allies which existed during World War I and World War II. Indeed, the military command structure of the Allied forces in Europe during World War II was the direct precursor of NATO's new military command structure. During World War II, General Dwight D. Eisenhower, who would become President of the United States in 1953, was the Supreme Commander of the Allied Forces in Europe, and his headquarters in southern England was known as Supreme Headquarters Allied Expeditionary Force. The combined Allied command structure provided decision-making groups that were in charge of shipping, munitions manufacturing, food, supplies, and also short- and long-term military planning. To be sure, there were conflicts among top Allied generals over strategies—where, how, and when to attack—and over the use

President Truman signs the NATO pact
in the presence of representatives
from countries in the Alliance.

of resources, but they were successfully resolved. The military command structure of NATO was, and is, the NATO Military Committee, composed of the military Chiefs of Staff of each member nation, except for France and Iceland. The Committee, which maintains a permanent international military staff, meets twice a year at the Supreme Headquarters Allied Powers of Europe (SHAPE), located first in Paris and since 1967 in Brussels, Belgium. The Military Committee and the combined allied forces are under the overall command of an American general; General Eisenhower was appointed the first Supreme Allied Commander of NATO in 1950.

The Atlantic Alliance was established primarily as a military defense organization, but its members also share broad, common political and economic goals. The agency which governs the political affairs and the everyday operations of the alliance is the NATO Council. It is composed of Permanent Representatives of all sixteen member nations. The Permanent Representatives maintain staffs made up of officials from the defense departments, treasuries, and foreign policy offices of each nation. The Council meets on a daily basis and in special situations is joined by Secretaries of State and Foreign Ministers.

The NATO Council oversees the vast network of NATO installations throughout Europe and North America, which include a permanent system of airfields, port facilities, storage depots, a complex communications and early warning radar system, military headquarters in several locations, and a 5,300-mile oil pipeline that extends from southern Italy to Belgium. The Council also funds such research projects as ocean floor exploration and grants university scholarships. In practical terms, this far-reaching organization makes it possible for Dutch pilots to fly British fighter planes out of an American airbase in West Germany.

While NATO does not have official provisions in its charter for unified political and economic action, its member nations are closely connected both politically and economically. With the exception of one member, Turkey, all NATO nations are democratic, Western societies. The unofficial economic arm of the alliance is known as the Organization for Economic Cooperation and Development (OECD). The OECD, composed of all sixteen NATO members and Australia, Austria, Finland, Ireland, New Zealand, Sweden, Switzerland, and Japan, keeps an eye on each member's economy, tries to harmonize economic and political policies, and settle trade and money problems. So, while alliance members have common war plans and hold common war maneuvers, they also try to respond to world developments in a unified voice.

Other important NATO agencies include the Nuclear Planning Group and the Nuclear Defense Affairs Committee, which decide on such issues as the storage of warheads, the placement of missiles in Europe, or the tactical use of battlefield nuclear weapons.

The spirit and tradition of cooperation from which NATO was founded was perhaps most eloquently described during World War II by Walter Lippmann, the famous American journalist, who wrote, "The Atlantic Ocean is not a frontier between Europe and the Americas. It is the inland sea of a community of nations allied with one another by geography, history, and vital necessity."

Indeed, the Truman Doctrine and the Marshall Plan were as President Truman remarked, "two halves of the same walnut." The Soviet domination of Eastern Europe, the Czech coup, and the Berlin blockade provided the keg of gunpowder while the complete failure of the United Nations as an effective peacekeeping organization was the spark which ignited the formation of the NATO alliance.

CHAPTER THREE

THE EARLY YEARS: TEMPORARY TROUBLES

T he political situation in Europe in 1949—at the birth of NATO—was confusing. Now, the United States and other Western countries were allied with their bitter enemy of five years earlier, Germany, and were adversaries of their former wartime ally, the Soviet Union. The United States was by far the greatest economic country in the world, and, with the Marshall Plan, Western Europe was on the path to rapid recovery from the war's ruination. The Soviet Union, refusing to allow self-determination in Eastern Europe, was cut off from American aid and instead had set out on its own austere recovery program. In 1952, Greece and Turkey became members of NATO, forming a strategic southeastern military flank in the eastern Mediterranean and on the border of the Soviet Union.

The first twenty years of the NATO alliance were characterized, in simplified terms, by a large European economic and military dependence on the United States. The Atlantic Alliance faced many challenges, both from without and within, which threatened its effectiveness as a unified and common defense organization. A majority of the troubles and crises of the early years were temporary. They were either resolved, or buried and forgotten. Other troubles, however, were far-reaching and permanent (they will be examined in later chapters). The old adage, "The only thing worse than dealing with allies is having no allies at all," would accurately describe the 1950s and 1960s of the NATO alliance.

Two main problem areas provided the NATO member nations with most of their internal difficulties during this early period. The first was that several West European (and finally the United States) required the use of defense forces and military operations outside of their native lands. The second issue centered on the notion that NATO was an alliance "among equals." While Article 6 of

28

the Treaty provided for a common defense of any member's overseas territories, the status of all such overseas territories was usually in flux; they were about to become independent nations. Great Britain, France, Belgium, and the Netherlands all held territories in either the Middle East or Africa. In 1946, the British who controlled Palestine (now Israel) came under criticism from the United States and France for their policy of stopping all Jewish refugee settlement in that territory. In Indonesia, Dutch troops engaged in "police actions" and outright military operations in 1948. The Dutch, trying to delay and block independence of Java and Sumatra, captured the anti-Communist leaders of the movement. In response, the United States condemned the Dutch actions at the United Nations and also temporarily suspended Marshall Plan economic aid to the Netherlands. This was perhaps the earliest use of economic sanctions against a NATO ally by the United States. In 1949, the Dutch relented and left Indonesia. The only active NATO support for the Dutch position came from Belgium.

In 1950, Communist North Korea attacked South Korea and under United Nations approval American troops were promptly sent to Korea to halt the Communist advance. The Soviet Union did not veto the action because they were boycotting the Security Council in protest over the United Nations refusal to give the Chinese seat on the Council, held by Chiang Kai-shek the Nationalist leader of Formosa, to Mao Tse-tung, the Communist leader of mainland China. After a series of victories and reversals, the commander of the American forces there, General Douglas MacArthur, began in 1951 to decisively push back the North Koreans and the Chinese, who had intervened on the North's side. MacArthur wanted to continue his counterinvasion and capture all of North Korea and perhaps more territory. President Truman, adhering to his own containment policy, ordered MacArthur to stop his assault in February 1951. Later, MacArthur was removed

Dutch troops take up a position
near the center of the Indonesian
city of Jakarta in 1948.

from his command by Truman for launching his counter-attack without authorization. But two processes were behind Truman's decision. There was considerable pressure from NATO allies both in and out of United Nations sessions to negotiate a peace settlement with North Korea. And it was clear to Truman that "liberating" North Korea and then moving against Communist China would be placing Asia first and Europe and NATO second in American foreign policy. Such a military action would require the removal of American troops from their NATO posts, leaving Europe exposed and vulnerable. In July 1951, hostilities cessated, and peace talks with North Korea and China began.

A prime example of internal NATO division focused on the issue of the rearmament of West Germany in 1953. Several NATO states which had been reduced to ruins by the German military in the war were opposed to rearming West Germany. American military planners realized, however, that to field the number of soldiers required to mount an effective and sizeable NATO conventional force (infantry, artillery, tanks, aircraft, etc.) they would have to draw them from Germany, the largest and most powerful industrial nation of Europe. Moreover, West Germany was situated in a strategic position, on the corridor between Western Europe and the Soviet Union. West Germany was also a highly desirable ally, with 95 percent of the vote against the German communists, unlike several other NATO states. In 1953, John Foster Dulles, the American Secretary of State, in an effort to promote more active European participation in its own defense, told the NATO allies that if a proposed French plan for a Europe-wide army failed, then American aid in Europe would be reappraised. The plan did fail, but instead of withdrawing American assistance, Dulles made it clear that in exchange for the continued American military guarantee to protect Western Europe, West Germany would have to be rearmed. In 1955, West Germany became a member of

NATO and began a program of rearmament. So much for the idea of an agreement "among equals."

The Suez Affair of 1956 was perhaps one of the most seriously divisive events of the early years of NATO. Since 1869, Great Britain and France had been in control of the Suez Canal which earned $25 million each year in profits. In 1955, Dulles, learning that Egypt had made a deal to buy arms from the Soviet Union, offered Gamel Abdel Nasser, the Egyptian president, American aid for the building of the Aswan Dam, an ambitious project designed to regulate the waters of the Nile. Nasser accepted the offer, but other circumstances upset the deal. Dulles, meeting Congressional opposition to the Egyptian aid package, delayed concluding the agreement. In the meantime, Nasser infuriated Dulles first by joining a military alliance with pro-Soviet Syria, and the anti-Western governments of Yemen and Jordan, and then by granting official recognition to Communist China, in place of the non-Communist Chinese government that had established itself on the island of Formosa (now Taiwan). In retaliation, Dulles abruptly withdrew the offer to support the construction of the Aswan Dam. Nasser immediately nationalized the Suez Canal, declaring it the legal property of the Egyptian government. Ironically, the last British troops had left the canal zone five weeks earlier. Britain and France, totally unprepared for this incident, reached a secret agreement with Israel (whose ships were being threatened by Egypt near the Sinai passage to the Red Sea) to mount a concerted attack against Egypt. In late October 1956, Israel attacked Egyptian army positions in the Sinai Peninsula while British and French forces landed near the canal, at Port Said.

For NATO, it was a disaster. The United States put tremendous pressure on the British and the French in emergency United Nations sessions. An American oil embargo was placed on them. More importantly, however, was the economic effect of American pressure on the Brit-

Guns of the Royal Navy are guarding British
ships that have just passed through the Suez
Canal, in the days before it was nationalized
by Egyptian President Gamel Nasser.

ish pound. Large quantities of sterling silver (on which its value was based) were sold by the United States, bringing down the value of the pound on the world currency market. Yielding to such pressures, after one week the British and French agreed to a ceasefire and then a withdrawal. They were hours away from capturing the Suez Canal. Years would pass before the United States, Great Britain, and France—the Big Three NATO members—would fully trust each other. It's possible that if they had consulted together before the Suez Affair, it could have been completely averted. Dulles did not notify Britain and France of the American decision to withdraw aid from Egypt, and France and Britain did not consult with the United States before embarking on their military expedition. The Anglo-French motives for the expedition, in addition to securing the canal for free navigation and access to the oil-rich Persian Gulf and for $25 million annual revenue, also concerned preserving their waning world prestige. Largely through the efforts of a NATO member, the United States, they didn't retake the canal, and instead of gaining prestige they were humiliated into accepting a ceasefire and a withdrawal.

There were obvious results of the Suez Affair—all presumptions of superpower status were removed from the British and the French (this Germany had already done in 1941), but there was also one serious hidden outcome of the bungled expedition. At the exact same time that the Suez Affair was happening, Soviet tanks rolled through the streets of Budapest, Hungary, putting down a widespread uprising against communist domination. In a week of fighting, it was estimated that 7,000 Soviet soldiers and 30,000 Hungarians died. The Soviets deviously timed their repressive military actions to occur behind the smokescreen of another event that held the world's attention, the Suez Affair (a practice that has become characteristic of the Soviet Union). When the United Nations Security Council met, it was to reproach Britain and France and resolve the Suez crisis. The Soviets' brutal repression of Hungary was mentioned, but it was secondary to Suez and also subject to the Soviet veto, according to Security Council procedures. Thus the United States and the other NATO nations let the opportunity to intervene in some way in (or even condemn) the Soviet action slip through their fingers. Instead, the Council's principal member, the United States, strongly condemned the Suez expedition—a political decision which must have seriously puzzled and upset the two other major NATO states, Great Britain and France.

Several other significant incidents cast serious doubt on whether or not a unified political vision of the world was shared among NATO members. During the 1950s, Tunisia and Morocco were French protectorates, and Algeria an outright French colonial territory. In these years, the French repeatedly rejected demands of independence from local leaders, particularly in Algeria which was a "department," or province, of France. In 1957, Tunisia and Morocco were granted independence, but in Algeria a widespread war of liberation was being waged against the French. In the following year, the United States and Great Britain sold and shipped arms to Tunisia, a most peculiar action for allies to take. Tunisia openly supported the Algerian partisans in their war of independence, and it was common knowledge that they would send these arms to the Algerian fighters. When the Anglo-American arms shipment became known, the French delegate left the regular NATO planning session in protest.

Disunity and disagreement were not, however, the only hallmarks of the NATO alliance. After World War II, the French were also engaged in a protracted military struggle against communist forces to maintain control of their colonies in Indochina, particularly Vietnam. In 1953, when General Dwight D. Eisenhower was elected President of the United States, Truman's containment policy was largely replaced with a more interventionist or active military-based policy. The full support of America and the NATO allies for the French actions in Vietnam was generously given, right up to the final French defeat at Dien Bien Phu in 1954. It is estimated that between 1950–1954 the United States provided $2.6 billion in military and economic aid to France in Vietnam, thus paying for nearly 80 percent of the entire war. When the French withdrew to South Vietnam after Dien Bien Phu, active NATO solidarity and support took the form of United States refusal to grant any concessions to the Vietnamese Communist leader, Ho Chi Minh, who had successfully driven out the French. Following the French defeat, Eisenhower acted swiftly to prevent all of Southeast Asia from falling into communist hands, according to his "domino theory" of conquest. Eisenhower explained his domino theory in a 1954 press conference by comparing all of Southeast Asia (Vietnam, Laos, Cambodia, Thailand, Burma, etc.) to a row of dominoes, going on to say that if one domino were knocked over, in effect, by violent communist overthrow, then surely the entire row would also quickly fall. In the meantime, a peace plan developed, by the French and Ho Chi Minh, without Eisenhower's knowledge, called for United Nations-sponsored elections in Vietnam. But the fear caused by the domino theory impelled Eisenhower to make the partition of the country permanent, support the corrupt government of Ngo Dinh Diem in the new South Vietnam, and ultimately send American troops to fight against Vietnamese liberation forces. To protect the threatened dominoes, Dulles set up another mutual defense association—the Southeast Asia Treaty Organization—SEATO—composed of Britain, France, Australia, New Zealand, Thailand, Pakistan, and the Philippines, and the United States. The treaty, a new example of the old containment policy, also contained a clause which brought South Vietnam under the protection of its members. Although the SEATO strategy was supposed to use treaty-member troops (British and French) and American economic aid and material to police threatened Southeast Asia, Dulles did not receive the cooperation of the British and French where the use of their soldiers was concerned.

In the late 1950s and through the 1960s, a variety of actions and events created situations which in some cases strengthened NATO unity, and in others damaged it. In 1955, the issue of German rearmament had been resolved among alliance members, and West Germany was admitted into NATO. West Germany's participation in the alliance greatly enhanced the political and military strength of NATO. The Soviets reacted to West Germany's entry into NATO by setting up a counter military alliance—the Warsaw Pact—formed by the Soviet Union, Poland, Czechoslovakia, East Germany, Hungary, Rumania, Bulgaria, and Albania. In 1958, a pro-Soviet military coup in neighboring Iraq toppled the pro-Western government and threatened to spill over into Lebanon. Anti-American sentiments led to anti-American rioting in Beirut, and Eisenhower sent 10,000 U.S. Marines into Lebanon in support of the government. American air bases in West Germany were used to stage the military operation without, however, first consulting the West German Chancellor, Konrad Adenauer. While this incident did not contribute to a climate of trust among the NATO allies, the British supported the American strategy of protecting pro-Western Arab governments by dropping 2,500 parachute troops into Jordan.

United States involvement in Vietnam, which rapidly expanded throughout the 1960s, created deep political rifts among the NATO allies, and had far-reaching repercussions for NATO unity. France's war in Algeria, which ended in Algerian independence in 1962, also found little support among the NATO allies, particularly with the United States. And it was in 1967 that the French president, Charles de Gaulle, severed relations with the NATO military command structure and struck out on his own political path.

The first twenty years of the NATO alliance were not predominately years of disunity and crisis. To paint such a portrait would be to provide a false image of the alliance in those years. Out of the chaos and rubble of war, NATO became a strongly unified alliance of nations in those twenty years. Greece, Turkey, and West Germany were brought into the alliance. The Marshall Plan was successful and West European economies were booming. And democratic governments were firmly established in all NATO countries, except in Turkey. Relations between NATO nations were, for the most part, as harmonious as could be expected from an alliance of independent, democratic states. The political and economic realities of the early years of the alliance, however, had changed drastically by the early 1970s. Political policies, military actions, and world-shaking events created tensions between the allies in the decade of the 1970s that would have far-reaching, and not temporary, consequences for NATO.

CHAPTER FOUR

DEEP STRAINS IN THE ALLIANCE

Since the end of World War II (1945), the United States' alliance with the West European nations —NATO—has been the foundation for most American foreign policy. Not only is NATO a military defense organization, but it is also a confederation of nations which share and cherish many values and traditions—democracy, free enterprise, a common cultural heritage, and close trade ties.

When NATO was formed in 1949, the United States was the single most dominant power in the world—both economically and militarily. At the war's end, it was estimated that the United States produced 50 percent of the world's goods, 45 percent of the world's arms, and two-thirds of all ships. In 1949, the United States was also the only nation to have exploded a nuclear bomb. Later in that year, the Soviets exploded a nuclear bomb, but nonetheless, by the 1960s, the United States still enjoyed a clearcut nuclear superiority over the Soviets. And the original pledge to defend Western Europe made by the United States was based on the American threat to use nuclear weapons in the event of a large-scale Soviet attack westward.

Conditions, however, have changed drastically since 1949. Western Europe is no longer characterized by weak and war-ravaged nations. Now, some European countries enjoy standards of living that are higher than those of the United States. More importantly, the American economy has seriously deteriorated over the past decade—the trade surpluses of the 1960s became the trade deficits of the 1970s. The enormous imbalance in economic strength that existed in 1949 between the United States and Western Europe no longer exists. Today, the American share of the production of the world's goods is down to 20 percent. And military realities have been transformed over the past thirty-five years, too. American guarantees to wreak nuclear destruction on the Soviet Union in the event of an invasion from the Soviet satellite-empire are no longer totally credible, or one-sided. The Soviets have achieved an approximate "parity" or equality in nuclear weaponry and could as well unleash their own forces of massive destruction on the United States.

Similarly, relations between East and West—between the NATO and Warsaw Pact countries—have also dramatically changed since the early days of the Atlantic Alliance. In some areas the "iron curtain" of Churchill's speech, designed to shut out all Western influences from Eastern Europe, has been partially lifted over the past twenty years. A great deal of trade and different degrees of scientific and technological cooperation now exist between NATO and Warsaw Pact nations.

Today, many foreign policy analysts believe that the difficulties and strains among the NATO members threaten to break the alliance apart, or at least to render it totally ineffective. The present problems within NATO are no longer only temporary trends based on international incidents or military actions. Instead, the present crises are tied to long-term policy differences and to deeply conflicting views. Three major issues disrupt the political unity of NATO and threaten its continued existence: (1) strategic nuclear parity and its consequences, (2) conflicting views of détente, and (3) economic rivalry between the United States and Western Europe, and "burden-sharing." This chapter and the two that follow will explore each of these issues separately and in detail.

STRATEGIC PARITY

The original purpose of the formation of the Atlantic Alliance was to safeguard Western Europe's security through an American "nuclear guarantee." Specifically, this meant that the United States would use its long-range nuclear weapons, if necessary, against any potential military aggression toward its Western allies. NATO's symbol of a shield with a sword thrusting up behind it captures this original defense idea. The shield, represented by American NATO troops stationed in Western Europe or, simply American military commitment, would provide safety behind which Europe could recover from the war and rebuild its economies and armies. The sword, represented by nuclear weapons, would guarantee the strength and impenetrability of the shield. In practice, this implied that if Europe were attacked by the Soviet Union or a Warsaw Pact country, NATO ground forces would defend the area—the shield—until U.S. Air Force long-range bombers or missiles—the sword—struck at targets in the Soviet Union. Thus, the very threat of using American nuclear weapons would deter any potential attack—a doctrine known as "deterrence."

In the first decade of NATO, the American nuclear guarantee was, for the most part, valid and effective. Truman, determined to halt any dreams of Soviet expansion in Europe, greatly expanded American military capacities through the early 1950s. Air bases from which U.S. Air Force long-range bombers could strike deep into the Soviet Union with atomic bombs were established in many NATO countries and in Japan and Korea. In 1945, the United States exploded its first atomic bomb and in that same year dropped two of them on Japan, ending the war that had begun for the United States with the Japanese surprise attack on Pearl Harbor in December 1941. Although the Soviets also exploded an atomic bomb in 1949, American nuclear superiority remained intact through the late 1960s and so did NATO's earliest defense policy of "the shield and the sword." By 1955, however, the Soviet Union had established the Warsaw Pact—their own military alliance, which included armed forces from all their East European satellite countries—and there were important changes in the American nuclear strategy.

Although NATO's conventional ground forces were small in comparison to the Soviet Red Army's, a limited Soviet ground attack on, for example, West Berlin would not bring an immediate nuclear bombing response. Such an "all-out" response would escalate the limited fighting to a nuclear war, and the Soviets would retaliate against Western Europe with their own nuclear bombs. To compensate for this problem, battlefield nuclear weapons, for example, nuclear artillery and tank shells were developed in the mid-1950s by the United States for possible use in such limited, conventional wars. John Foster Dulles, the Secretary of State under Eisenhower, used the nuclear threat to break up and go beyond the postwar containment policy. Dulles' confrontational style of handling international crises became known as "brinksmanship," a term taken from a 1956 *Life* magazine article in which he was interviewed. In the magazine he remarked that:

> You have to take chances for peace, just as you must take chances for war . . . The ability to get to the verge of the war without getting into the war is the necessary art . . . If you try to run away from it, if you are scared to go to the brink, you are lost . . . We walked to the brink and looked it in the face.

In 1961, John F. Kennedy became president, and in 1962, the Soviet attempt to install nuclear weapons in Cuba, the Cuban missile crisis, convinced him to launch a major American nuclear arms buildup. By 1967, the American nuclear arsenal included 67 Polaris submarines capable of carrying 656 missiles, 600 long-range bombers, and 1,000 I.C.B.M.'s (Intercontinental Ballistic Missiles) or long-range missiles. Reacting to the loss of world prestige over the Cuban missile crisis and to the American buildup, the Soviets embarked on their own nuclear arms buildup. In 1962, the Soviets had only 70 I.C.B.M.'s, by 1965 they had 220, and by 1972 over 1,000. Therefore, America's strategic nuclear superiority (that is, the greater number of long-range missiles and warheads) had eroded by the beginning of the 1970s. The new relationship between American and Soviet nuclear forces was one of "strategic parity," or of equality in numbers. Approximate strategic nuclear parity still exists today and has been one of the chief causes of disruption among the NATO allies for the past six years.

Since the original NATO defense concept was based on American strategic nuclear superiority and since the Soviets have achieved rough strategic parity, it follows that the original NATO plan is no longer completely valid. Here is a hypothetical scenario illustrating the problem posed by strategic parity: Warsaw Pact conventional forces (tanks, artillery, and infantry) suddenly attack West Germany but halt their advance after half a day of fighting. In this half day, they have captured and secured one small area of the country. NATO conventional forces cannot repel the unexpected attack and are forced to pull back. But the Warsaw Pact forces do not advance; instead they dig in, consolidating their small gains. In this situation it is unthinkable that the United States would launch I.C.B.M.'s from the United States against the Soviet Union. Such an action would precipitate an all-out nuclear war because the Soviets would respond with their own missile attack against the United States. Thus, the American "nuclear guarantee" as it exists now, represents a potentially dangerous situation for the United States. In plain terms, would or should the United States risk nuclear annihilation for the sake of protecting Western Europe? How can NATO upgrade its defense strategy? This is one of the questions which seriously threatens NATO's unity and future existence.

Possible solutions to the problem of nuclear parity

exist, but not a single one appeals to both Americans and Europeans. The United States under President Reagan wants to place intermediate-range nuclear missiles in West Germany to solve part of the problem. These missiles—Pershing II's and cruise missiles—with a range of more than 1,500 miles are capable of striking deep into the Soviet Union. Having these missiles in Western Europe, the Reagan Administration argues, would provide Europe with its own nuclear guarantee. Then the Europeans, particularly the West Germans, need not worry about the credibility of the American guarantee to use I.C.B.M.'s to protect Europe. Moreover, the supporters of this argument continue, the Pershing II's will also balance the 300 new Soviet medium-range missiles (SS-20's) targeted in 1982 on Western Europe, for which there is no NATO counterpart. If the Pershing II missiles are placed in West Germany, the Netherlands, Italy, Belgium, and Britain, they could prevent the Soviets from blackmailing Western Europe by threatening a separate European nuclear war and thus driving a wedge between the United States and its European NATO allies.

The debate over the deployment of the Pershing II's has become a test of NATO's unity. Many Europeans do not want NATO nuclear weapons installed in their countries. Great Britain and France are the only West European nations to have their own nuclear weapons (and France is not in the NATO military structure). Massive antinuclear demonstrations—by up to 400,000 people—in Holland and West Germany preceded President Reagan's visit to West Germany in the summer of 1982. The demonstrators specifically opposed the West German government's acceptance of the Pershing II's. Although the demonstrations did include a majority of genuine antinuclear groups, there were also many groups involved for self-promoting motives—groups seeking the reunification of the two Germanies, and also several pro-Soviet German Communist Party groups. In an address to his nation in Novem-

ber 1983, François Mitterand, the President of France, summarized the official French position on the Europe-wide demonstrations by remarking that over the past decade, "the East has developed missiles and the West has developed pacifists."

Ironically, however, it was the Europeans who asked for the American medium-range missiles in the first place. In 1977, Helmut Schmidt, then the West German Chancellor, expressed concern over the link between Western Europe's defense and the American strategic nuclear deterrent. The Dutch also asked the United States to place the new missiles in Europe, and in 1979 NATO decided to do so, with deployment scheduled for, and subsequently begun in late 1983. NATO's plan called for installing 112 cruise missiles in Italy; 48 each in Belgium and the Netherlands; 160 in Great Britain; and in West Germany, NATO's central front, 96 cruise missiles and 108 Pershing missiles. Besides offering Western Europe a counterbalance to the numerical superiority of Warsaw Pact conventional ground forces, the "Euromissiles," as they are often called, would also press the Soviets to seriously consider nuclear arms limitation talks and would demonstrate European military solidarity. The negative public response, however, led to bitter political debates which in late 1982 cost Schmidt his position as Chancellor of West Germany. In his November 1983 address to the French people, François Mitterand declared the Euromissile crisis to be

*Antinuclear demonstrators in
West Germany protest deployment
of Pershing II missiles by forming
a human chain 67 miles (108 km)
long between the United States
forces' headquarters in Stuttgart
and the army's Wiley barracks
at Neu Ulm.*

47

"the most serious since the blockade of Berlin in 1948 and the Cuban missile crisis of 1962."

Many Europeans fear that the presence of nuclear weapons on their soil risks turning their nations into battlefields where limited nuclear wars may be fought. Presumably, a losing conventional war would invite use of short-range nuclear weapons (artillery and tank shells, for example) and then if necessary, the deep-penetrating, medium-range Pershing II's and cruise missiles. Ultimately, American strategic (long-range) nuclear weapons could be used. Some Europeans even suspect that the United States wants to deploy the medium-range missiles in Europe (the short-range systems have been there for decades) so that if a war does break out, a limited nuclear war can be confined to Europe—without involving American strategic missiles. It is precisely for this reason—the noninvolvement of American nuclear forces—that the Soviets do not want the Pershing II's to be deployed in Western Europe. President Reagan did nothing to remove these fears when he remarked offhandedly in a press conference in 1982 that in the event of an attack, a limited nuclear war in Europe was a possibility. He later assured the European press that if a NATO ally faced such a dire situation, it would also automatically involve the United States.

Another and perhaps the most acceptable alternative to compensate for the problem of Soviet strategic nuclear parity is the strengthening of NATO's West European conventional ground forces, which are vastly outnumbered in firepower—in tanks, artillery, and combat aircraft. A strong, conventional ground force can defend territory effectively enough so that a nuclear response would not be necessary in all but the gravest situation. General Bernard Rogers, the Supreme Commander of NATO, outlined the problems created by insufficient conventional forces in terms of the NATO doctrine of "flexible response." Flexible response is a three-layered defense posture:

(1) direct defense to defeat an attack or place the burden of escalation on the enemy,

(2) deliberate escalation, and

(3) nuclear response, the ultimate guarantee.

Given the present imbalance between NATO and Warsaw Pact conventional forces, NATO's defensive actions could degenerate quickly to the second level, and then failing that, to the third. A successfully waged conventional war thus provides a buffer between levels 2 and 3, and the Reagan Administration is emphasizing the need for a conventional military buildup among NATO allies for the fighting of a conventional long war. Recent debates within the alliance have indicated, however, that most West European nations are unwilling to finance increased military requirements, conventional or nuclear. It should also be noted that some foreign policy analysts feel that statistics comparing NATO and Warsaw Pact forces are not truly representative. They point out, for example, that while the pact has 150 percent more tanks, 180 percent more artillery, and 15 percent more combat aircraft in Europe, the number of NATO soldiers is comparable to the pact's. Regardless of statistical imbalances in certain conventional forces areas, the question of the Pershing II deployment in Western Europe still remains foremost. If the NATO nations which asked for the United States development and deployment of the new missiles endlessly delay their decisions or reject their pledges to deploy, then the United States may question its desire to continue in an alliance of prosperous Western nations which are unwilling to bear the full burden of responsibility—economic, military and psychological—for their own defense. Deployment of a handful of the missiles began in early 1984 in West Germany and Italy, but thus far not in other NATO nations. American policy makers may ask themselves: Is a Western Europe that won't defend itself worth defending?

Thus far, the strategic nuclear parity-Euromissile issue has become a symbol for NATO disunity. It threatens to separate the United States from Western Europe politically.

In the following chapter we'll look at the second major divisive issue confronting NATO: détente.

CHAPTER FIVE

DÉTENTE WITH THE SOVIETS: CONFLICTING VIEWS

Détente is a French word which in international politics refers to a relaxing or easing of tensions between nations. In recent years it has been used to describe a relaxation in the relationship between the West and the Soviet Union. Conflicting views on the degree of détente with the Soviets is perhaps the most far-reaching of the difficulties among NATO member nations today.

Détente with the Soviets is a process which has been on-again, off-again since the first "summit conference" in Geneva, Switzerland, in 1954, attended by representatives of the United States, the Soviet Union, Great Britain, France, and other countries. In practice, détente has meant cooperation between NATO countries and the Soviet Union (and Warsaw Pact countries) in the areas of arms control, trade, and science and technology. The deep, present problem between the United States and many of its West European NATO allies centers on disagreements over the long-term effects of détente on NATO political solidarity and military effectiveness. There are extremely divergent views among NATO countries about Soviet intentions toward Western Europe. Many West European governments claim that a high degree of détente is desirable because it is beneficial to their economies, opening up trade markets with Soviet-bloc countries. Détente also works toward their longstanding dream of a united Europe. An easing of tensions with the Soviets is customarily rewarded by a variety of Soviet concessions on opening up Eastern Europe. The Reagan Administration believes that some measure of détente is useful but that the level détente has reached in Western Europe since the early 1970s is alarming and dangerous. This is so, they would argue, because the Soviets want to dominate Western Europe gradually by influencing European national elections, by supporting West European Communist parties, and by developing trade and energy resource dependencies—so that Western Europe needs East European markets and Soviet natural gas and oil. Thus, by becoming so deeply involved at all levels of West European society the Soviets may, in the words of one policy expert, be able "to take over Europe without firing a single shot." To understand these different views of the dangers of détente we must first investigate the process that led up to this deep political conflict among NATO allies.

From the first summit conference in 1954 to the early 1970s, détente between the United States and the Soviet Union was completely upset from time to time by actions, incidents, and policies of both superpowers. In June 1961, President John F. Kennedy met with the Soviet head of state, Nikita S. Khrushchev, in Vienna to discuss ways of peaceful cooperation, nuclear testing limitations, and the question of free access between the divided city of Berlin.

For a decade, millions of refugees fled East Germany through the border between East Berlin and West Berlin. With this flood of refugees, East Germany was losing its most valuable human resources, its young population. Over the years, half of the refugees were under twenty-five years of age, and a quarter were between twenty-five and forty-five years of age. In addition, many of the refugees were highly skilled technicians. It was estimated that in six months of 1961 alone, nearly 300,000 people escaped to the West through West Berlin. Kennedy and Khrushchev could not, however, reach any agreement either on arms limitations, the status of Berlin, or on the settlement of war reparations from Germany. In August 1961, Khrushchev had a concrete and barbed wire wall constructed around the entire city of East Berlin to stop the river of East Germans which was steadily flowing to the West. This act of Soviet aggression violated the Vienna talks and destroyed hopes for détente.

Tensions between the United States and the Soviet Union worsened in 1962, when Khrushchev attempted to deploy medium-range missiles on the island of Cuba, ninety miles off the tip of Florida. Kennedy surrounded Cuba with U.S. Navy warships, prepared 12,000 Marines for an invasion of the island, and put American I.C.B.M.'s on alert. This "brinksmanship" created an intense nuclear war scare in the United States for nearly two weeks. Eventually, the Soviets removed the missile launching sites in return for an American assurance that Cuba would not be invaded.

There were also several relatively minor instances of American troublemaking which upset the process of détente. From 1964 to 1966, when Lyndon B. Johnson was president, pro-Soviet governments in Brazil, Greece, and Indonesia were overthrown, in a period when the secret, behind-the-scenes operations of the Central Intelligence Agency (CIA) were frequently employed. In 1965, Johnson sent U.S. Marines to the Dominican Republic to stabilize a government threatened by a leftist overthrow. While West European NATO allies supported the United States in many of these less ambitious actions, they realized that in the Cuban missile crisis the United States would go to war, perhaps nuclear war, without first consulting its allies.

Perhaps this realization was what partially motivated Charles de Gaulle, the French president, to lead France into a separate relationship of détente with the Soviet Union in the mid-1960s. In 1966, de Gaulle withdrew the French from the Military Command Structure of NATO and ordered all allied NATO forces out of France. France did remain in the political (NATO Council) and economic (OECD) agencies of NATO, and it did remain in NATO's early warning radar and communications network. In a separate defense agreement with West Germany, France kept its NATO troops in that country. It wasn't until 1974 that France finally agreed to compensate the United States for the military bases that were taken over by the French as a result of this withdrawal. At the time, de Gaulle was much criticized for his independent posture vis-à-vis defense and détente. De Gaulle also set France on a course of independent military defense, which has been well achieved—precisely the original purpose of NATO. France subsequently developed its own nuclear arms program outside of NATO and had varying degrees of success in its separate détente with the Soviets. Ironically, France which is now led by a Socialist president, François Mitterand, has become one of America's most reliable and most responsible NATO allies.

Today the deepest conflict over détente within NATO exists, however, between the United States and West Germany. West Germany seeks greater cooperation with the Soviets in the hopes of expanding political, cultural, scientific, and commercial ties with its sister state, East Germany. West Germany has pursued détente vigorously since 1970, when it signed the Soviet-German Agreement recognizing the western border of Poland, and hence the eastern border of East Germany. Détente is highly desired by the West Germans because they have a great general interest in expanding trade and economic ties with Eastern Europe and a specific interest in the reunification of the two Germanies. Without détente the Soviet leaders will not allow East Germany to participate in any West-oriented cultural associations, and will not allow a relatively open border between West and East Berlin to exist, which enables relatives to visit each other. Clearly, West Germans are also justifiably concerned with détente since their country sits in the heart of the invasion route between Western and Eastern Europe. West and East Germany are linked by a common history, a common language and shared customs, and also by widespread trade arrangements. The Soviets allow East Germans to participate in the West German antinuclear peace movement, but do not allow antinuclear demonstrations in East Germany which are aimed at

Soviet or Warsaw Pact policies. In this respect, détente is a one-way street, enabling East Germany to participate in the affairs of West Germany but preventing any similar Western, democratic liberties in the East.

Indeed, it should be noted that Western Europe's greater reliance on détente in the past decade may have been partially caused by American policies. In the early 1970s, United States policy largely ignored Europe and instead was focused on the Vietnam War and on establishing strong trade ties with Japan and China. America's military involvement in Vietnam in the late 1960s and early 1970s also created great divisions between it and other NATO allies. More importantly, the prestige, world image, and economic power of the United States was severely damaged by the Vietnamese war. The United States itself was deeply divided over the war in Vietnam, which took over 50,000 American soldiers' lives and many more Vietnamese lives. Most NATO allies did not support the war, which was fought to support Eisenhower's domino theory of the early 1950s. Finally, the Watergate Scandal of 1973—when President Richard M. Nixon illegally tried to cover up his knowledge of illegal and dirty presidential compaign methods and was forced by Congress to resign—gave Europeans serious doubts about the United States willingness to defend Europe, or its ability to shape cogent and reliable foreign policies.

Under the Reagan Administration, the United States seriously distrusts Soviet desires for a broadened détente, believing that the Soviets do whatever they please within their sphere of influence, regardless of Western opinion. And indeed, the Soviets have used considerable force for their expansion into various parts of the world, and to maintain their own dominance in Eastern Europe. A partial list of Soviet misdeeds vastly overshadows the customary Soviet facades of cooperation and friendship. The list suggests the overall failure of détente, particularly from 1968 onward:

East German soldiers, with dogs and submachine guns,
guard workers who are repairing a stretch of rail
that passes through West Germany—a grim
reminder of the division between the two
Germanies, in spite of their common heritage,
and their recent efforts toward détente.

1946— Soviets attempt to "expand" into Greece, Turkey, and Iran.

1948— The Berlin blockade.

1953— Widescale riots against Soviet-installed communist government in East Germany put down by Soviet tanks and troops.

1956— (Budapest) Hungary tries to withdraw from Warsaw Pact and reform its Soviet-installed government. Popular uprising put down by Soviet forces—30,000 Hungarians dead, the new Prime Minister executed; 140,000 Hungarians flee the country; borders sealed by Soviets.

1961— Berlin wall erected by Soviets.

1962— Soviets attempt to install missiles in Cuba.

1968— Soviet forces put down "democratic socialism" reforms in Czechoslovakia, imprison popular leader, Alexander Dubcek.

1973— Soviets break agreement and massively supply Egypt with arms, and operate radar and missile systems for war with Israel.

1977— Soviets deploy 20,000 "surrogate" Cuban troops in Angola (Africa) to tilt civil war to Communists.

1978— Soviet advisors and 10,000 Cuban "surrogate" troops in Ethiopia to fight Somalia (Africa) and secure air and naval bases near the Persian Gulf.

1979— 85,000 Soviet soldiers invade Afghanistan and install unpopular Communist government.

1981— Soviets pressure Poland to end all democratization processes, ban the "Solidarity" union, and impose martial law.

1983— Soviets shoot down an unarmed Korean Airlines commercial passenger plane which

strays into Soviet airspace. Shot down outside Soviet airspace after being followed for
two hours by Soviet fighter jets—269 pas-
sengers dead.

Soviet military involvement in Africa and its invasion of
Afghanistan has sharpened the conflict over the views of
détente held by many West European NATO allies and
the United States. As a result of the recent Soviet military
operations, the United States has completely reevaluated
its views and policies of détente with the Soviet Union and
has placed emphasis on meeting Soviet challenges with
strong political and economic measures, and if necessary
with military intervention. Western Europe, with the possible exception of Great Britain, France, and to an extent,
Italy, seems unwilling to change its views on détente with
the Soviet Union.

Several policy analysts have remarked that there is a
struggle going on for the political orientation of Western
Europe, particularly for West Germany—between NATO
(the West) and the Warsaw Pact (the East). The Soviets
presumably want to politically detach or "decouple" West
Germany from NATO, while the Americans want to bring
it more deeply into NATO's defense system with the
deployment of the new medium-range missiles. The struggle for the future of Europe is going on. A neutralized
West Germany and a completely isolated United States
would be disastrous for NATO.

In the following chapter we'll examine the issue of eco-
nomic rivalry between the United States and Western
Europe. We'll also see how cooperation in trade between
NATO countries and Warsaw Pact countries has adverse-
ly affected the unity and effectiveness of the Atlantic
Alliance.

CHAPTER SIX

ECONOMIC RIVALRY, ECONOMIC DEPENDENCE

The Marshall Plan worked well in helping a war-shattered Europe to its feet. In the late 1940s, Western Europe's nations were just recovering from near bankruptcy and the United States was the world's only economic power. The United States share of world industrial production was nearly 50 percent after the war. Now, however, the American share of world production is only 20 percent. Moreover, while the American economy has been on the decline, the West European economies, when compared to their immediate postwar condition, have grown—although they seem to have stagnated in the early 1980s. In 1983, the *combined* Gross National Products (GNP), which are similar to national incomes, of Western Europe's nations was higher than that of the United States.

A prime example of the shift in the Western economic balance from the United States to Western Europe is best illustrated by comparing levels of production. One of the most important Europe-wide groups to apply for economic aid in 1949 under the Marshall Plan was the European Coal and Steel Community (ECSC), which was the forerunner of the present, powerful West European economic union, the European Economic Community (EEC) or Common Market, as it is also known. In 1953, the ECSC produced 36.8 million tons of steel, while the United States produced 101.2 million tons, and the Soviets produced 38.1 million tons. By the late 1970s, however, it was estimated that West European steel production had sharply risen to 132.4 million tons, while American production had only slightly risen to 132 million tons. In this period, Soviet production rose to 136 million tons, and Japanese production rose from 7.6 to 117 million tons between 1953 and 1976. Of the combined West European steel production in the late 1970s, West Germany accounted for some 53.5 million tons. In general trade, the American share of world exports (defined simply as goods sold in other countries) declined from almost 17 percent in 1950 to 14 percent by 1971, while EEC exports rose from just over 15 percent to nearly 29 percent in the same period. The American trade surplus of the 1940s and 1950s is now a trade deficit (meaning that America sells more goods and services abroad than it buys from other countries). The weak and bankrupt economies of postwar Western Europe became prosperous in the 1960s and 1970s. Indeed, the standard of living in many West European countries is comparable to that of the United States; in West Germany it is even higher. Recently, these vastly changed economic circumstances and the question of who pays for West European military defense have had a great negative impact on NATO.

Two principal issues are involved in the economic disagreements that seriously divide the NATO allies today. The first is the issue of "burden sharing," or of what percentage of their gross national product each nation earmarks for military defense, specifically for the defense of Western Europe. The second, and the more serious, issue involves competition for trade between the United States and its European allies, and cooperation in trade with the Soviet Union and other Warsaw Pact countries.

BURDEN SHARING

Since the beginning of NATO, the United States has carried the single largest burden of any NATO nation in financing NATO's military requirements. During the 1940s, 1950s and into the early 1960s, this oversized burden was acceptable because the United States was still far stronger economically than its European allies. Now, however, the economic balance has changed and the United States still carries a disproportionately large share of the military burden of NATO. The problem with this disproportion is that the United States and Western Europe (par-

ticularly West Germany) are now economic rivals, competing against each other to sell products within their own countries and vying for foreign markets all over the world. In 1980, the United States spent roughly 5.5 percent of its gross national product on defense, while its thirteen NATO allies spent an average of 4 percent (for example, West Germany, 3.2%; France, 3.9%; and the Netherlands, 3.4%). Only Great Britain spent almost as much as the United States on defense, some 5.1 percent of its gross national product. All in all, the United States spends nearly 25 percent more than its NATO allies on defense. Moreover, the Reagan Administration plans to devote 7.4 percent of the American gross national product to military defense spending in 1984, which would place an even heavier burden of over 40 percent of NATO's military budget on the United States. In 1950, taking on the major share of the NATO defense budget was acceptable, as Western Europe was recovering from war damage. But now with the complete recovery and great growth of Western Europe's economies, there is no legitimate reason why the United States should exceed its European allies in financing NATO. Critics question the value of the United States remaining in a military alliance whose prosperous nations will not equitably share the financial military burden.

The deliberations among NATO countries over who pays for and controls the controversial Pershing II and ground-based cruise missiles provides an excellent closeup

In West Germany's steel-producing Ruhr Valley, Europe's largest blast furnace stands as testament to the economic recovery that has made West Germany the most prosperous nation in Europe.

view of the issue of burden sharing. In December 1979, in responding to European queries over who would control the firing of the Pershing II missiles, the United States offered to set up a "dual-key" system. This meant that the launchers would be owned and controlled by the host NATO country and the warheads would be owned and controlled by the United States. Given past NATO policies, the host country controlling the launcher would also pay for its construction. In West Germany, a "single key" arrangement was immediately opted for since identifying the missile systems entirely with the United States would help to avoid internal political problems caused by various opponent groups and parties. In the end, however, cost was the determining factor, and all host countries chose the "single-key" plan in which the United States provided both launcher and warhead. Apart from the obvious problem with this arrangement—which is that the United States pays the entire bill for an updated West European defense system—there's also a more important problem. This more pressing problem is that every dollar spent on military defense represents a diversion of resources away from vital civilian sector needs—educational and social reforms, increase of foreign trade, reduction of taxes, and a general rise in the standard of living. To several foreign policy analysts, this diversion of resources is precisely why West European governments will not increase their military spending and build large, conventional ground forces, which would defuse the Euromissile debate considerably. For the United States, this deflection of vital resources into the military arena translated in 1981 into only $81 billion for the support of 350,000 American troops in Western Europe. Removing half of these troops, some critics suggest, would save the United States some $30 billion a year. European critics would probably say, in response to this issue of burden sharing, that the United States has much wider military ambitions throughout the world than Western Europe, hence the imbalance. We will examine this idea of global versus regional concerns in the final chapter.

Worldwide economic competition between the United States and Western Europe, particularly West Germany, exists in all types of industries: microelectronics, bioengineering, pharmaceuticals, industrial machinery, and arms, to name but a few areas. Aircraft and arms sales capture the essence of inter-NATO economic competition. In 1975, American combat aircraft manufacturers—General Dynamics, Lockheed, and Northrup—competed with Dassault, the French firm, which makes the Mirage jet fighter, for a large NATO contract. After months of deliberation, friendly persuasion, and perhaps questionable conduct, four NATO nations—Belgium, Denmark, the Netherlands, and Norway—placed orders for the General Dynamics F-16 fighter. In the area of commercial aircraft, there has also been much heated and bitter competition between the American Boeing Company and the European Airbus Company. (The Airbus Company is operated jointly by several West European companies and partially subsidized by their governments.) And arms sales throughout the developing world—Latin America, Africa, and the Middle East—provide perhaps the most severe competition of all among NATO countries. American, French, British, West German, Belgian, Italian, French-German, and French-British products all compete fiercely to corner the biggest part of the seemingly insatiable world market for rifles, missiles, tanks, aircraft, ships, and helicopters. Quarrelsome economic competition does not strengthen NATO unity or contribute to allied trust.

EAST-WEST TRADE

The most serious economic issue dividing NATO, however, is the role played by East-West trade in the security of the Western alliance. To the Americans, West European security and defense are undermined by excessive dependency on trade with the Soviet Union and other Warsaw Pact countries. To the Europeans, trade with their East European neighbors is a desirable, stabilizing force in international politics. The United States over the past decade has tended to focus on the military significance of trading with the Soviets—by restricting high technology products useable for defense systems. West Germany, for example, has tended to view such trade as the best way of maintaining a cultural and commercial bridge to its sister-state, East Germany. But does trade with the Soviet Union and other Pact countries affect Western security?

There is considerable evidence that ten years of economic cooperation with the Soviet Union and the Soviet-bloc nations has led the NATO countries into a trap in which they cannot retaliate economically against the Soviet Union for invading Afghanistan, for cracking down on Poland, or for the missile-destruction of the Korean Airlines passenger jet without damaging themselves economically. This economic dependency faces both the United States and West European countries, although for the West European countries, and West Germany in particular, the problem is far more acute. West Germany, the United States' most important NATO ally and most important economic rival, depends on the Soviet Union for trade links with East Germany. West Germany is clearly, as analysts report, the Soviet Union's largest Western trading partner. German trade with the Soviets rose sixfold between 1970 and 1980.

As of late 1983, trade with West Germany accounted for two-thirds of East Germany's trade with the West, and in early 1984, all signs indicated that West Germany was expanding its role in supporting the economy of East Germany. Trade between the two Germanies increased 8.5 percent during 1983, for a total of $6 billion, while West Germany's overall growth in trade with other nations was

2.3 percent. In the same year West Germany loaned East Germany nearly $400 million as trade widened into electric components, steel, trucks, and heavy machinery.

Today, the Soviet Union and the other Warsaw Pact nations owe such vast amounts of money to Western nations that a default or a failure to repay a loan or a credit would have serious consequences for several large Western banking systems. Failure to repay a large debt could bankrupt the loaning institutions. In a sense, it is impossible to call on or demand payment for a trade debt or loan, for there is no real alternative to nonpayment. The total combined debt of the Soviet Union and its pact nations to the West is estimated at $90 billion, up from approximately $6 billion in 1971. By 1985, it is expected to reach $140 billion. Immense credit subsidies and in some cases, unusual repayment practices and schedules have made such trade possible. Credit subsidies are basically government or bank-supported rates of interest which make credit cheaper to the borrower than it would normally be. These "credits," essentially, enable the Soviets to purchase Western goods far more cheaply than is usually possible.

Poland, by far the most indebted Pact country, offers a revealing example of NATO's inability or unwillingness to act in a united way toward Soviet violations of East-West agreements. When the Soviets crushed public freedoms in Poland by forcing the Polish government to declare martial law in the winter of 1981, the United States later announced that it was taking punitive economic measures against the Soviet Union: declaring a grain embargo, ceasing scientific and technological exchanges, and forbidding all American companies from working on or supplying the 3,700-mile Soviet-Siberian gas pipeline. The Reagan Administration then asked and finally tried to bully its European NATO allies—by stopping shipments of American parts used in European machinery—to also stop supplying vital components for the pipeline which would carry Soviet natural gas into Western Europe.

69

The $10 billion pipeline deal, however, provided West German, French, British, Italian, and Canadian industries with exciting economic opportunities in a time of deep economic troubles. West Germany, for instance, contracted to manufacture most of the steel pipe and to provide most of the engineering know-how for the project. Reagan's economic sanctions, however, were met with allied opposition from all but Great Britain. The pipeline sanctions were used by the United States as a test of NATO's ability to arrive at a common long-term economic approach to the Soviet pressure on Poland and possibly to any future Soviet military interventions. Later, in the summer of 1982, President Reagan provided the NATO allies with contradictory and confusing signals by giving the Soviet Union a one-year extension on grain trade, a prelude to the lifting of all American sanctions.

At the end of the pipeline affair, the damage done to NATO unity was clearly far greater than any damage or delays to the Soviet Union's natural gas project. American signals to their NATO allies were too confusing and too righteous. For example, at the same time that the Reagan Administration asked its alliance partners to boycott the Soviet pipeline, a contract between the Soviets and the American company, International Harvester, for heavy construction vehicles was not cancelled. And the grain embargo was lifted while the United States was still asking Western Europe to comply with trade sanctions. The Soviets have been importing grain since 1963 and obtain 65

This gas pipeline, designed to carry natural gas from the Soviet Union to Western Europe has focused attention on differences among the NATO allies.

percent of their total grain needs from the West. The imported grain is used to enrich the Soviets' diets and increase their livestock herds; thus the grain embargo could have posed a serious economic threat, but alternate suppliers existed in Argentina and Australia. Not only was NATO in disunity and disagreement over the grain embargo-trade sanction issue, but other sources for these products existed, making the tough American stance an empty gesture. In the summer of 1983, the United States again contradicted its own policies by making a $10 billion grain deal with the Soviet Union, agreeing to sell the Soviets a guaranteed 10 billion tons a year for five years. Whether due to the demands of American farmers or to the necessities of presidential elections, the Reagan Administration was also clearly unwilling to make an economic sacrifice, for losing American business interests for the purpose of taking tough measures against the Soviets would not garner many votes. In any case, all pipeline sanctions were lifted by late 1983. The crackdown on Poland and the Soviet pipeline embargo was a symbol of the Atlantic Alliance's disunity and of its overall immobility to act as a group.

Most ironically, the object of all this Western concern, Poland, was heavily in debt to the United States, West Germany, and other NATO countries. So, while the Soviets moved to crush Polish attempts to democratize their country, the West economically supported the nation. If the Western alliance nations had called in their loans, Poland could have been forced into national bankruptcy and the Western, mostly German, banks which made the loans would have forced serious trouble and perhaps collapse. Today, Poland's combined debt to Western alliance countries is estimated at $28.5 billion and will be nearly $33 billion by the end of 1985. The Soviet Union has a $9.6 billion debt to the West and anticipates an income of $8 billion a year from Western Europe for using the Soviet natural gas pipeline. What worries many foreign policy analysts is that this kind of trade détente is another one-way street—beneficial to the Soviets and the Soviet-bloc countries but of doubtful and even harmful value to NATO nations.

Trade dependency, especially on such vital resources as oil and natural gas, may provide a means of dominating Western Europe alliance nations without firing a shot through the process known as "Finlandization." This process refers to the way in which Soviet desires and policies gradually but steadily gained dominance over the Soviets' small, democratic neighbor, Finland. Finland, which now depends on the Soviet Union for oil, is also linked closely by trade with the Soviet Union which is, in fact, Finland's single largest trading partner. Finlandization is the formation of economic and political policies that are suitable to Soviet interests. It is a slow, long-term method for achieving economic domination. A prime example of this process can be seen in Finland's 1983 United Nations vote to condemn the United States for its invasion of Grenada, while in 1980, it abstained from voting to condemn the Soviet Union in the United Nations for its much larger, more brutal invasion of Afghanistan.

In contrast to the United States, which is relatively self-sufficient, Western Europe is highly dependent on such vital external resources as oil from the Middle East, gas from the Soviet Union, and food from a variety of nations. There is more than ample evidence of the vulnerabilities of Western economies to overextended Soviet and Eastern-bloc trade. The pipeline crisis did not result in a neutralized Western Europe and an isolated United States, but it stood as a clear example of the interdependence of the world's economies. Most importantly, it emphasized the urgent need for and lack of a united NATO position on the role of politics in East-West trade.

CHAPTER SEVEN

A NEW ATLANTICISM, NEW FRONTIERS

T he ancient Greek philosopher, Aristotle, wrote that the only certainty in life is change itself. People change, neighborhoods and governments change, and so do friendships, partnerships, and alliances. One's former ally can suddenly become one's future adversary—for example, the United States and the Soviet Union in the postwar 1940s. Accordingly, the NATO alliance, the foundation for West European security for almost forty years can and should also change. The direction that such changes take will determine the future of the Atlantic Alliance. Political leaders and the voting public of NATO countries will have to address the question of whether or not NATO will or should exist in the near future, and if so what form it will take.

Indeed, disagreement and diversity of opinion is built into the very nature of the Atlantic Alliance because it is a confederation of free, democratic, and independent nations—unlike the Warsaw Pact which is a compulsory association of subjugated, communist states. Incidents and crises have upset the equilibrium of NATO during the past, but the present dilemma has been caused by widely divergent ways of looking at long-term economic and political issues. The NATO of the 1980s is operating as if the political, economic, and military realities of the mid-1950s existed. The overwhelming economic dominance in the world that the United States enjoyed from 1945 onward has ended. By the early 1970s, the full recovery of the Western European industrial nations from the devastation of World War II was complete. Politically, the 1970s also marked a period of détente, an easing of cold war tensions between the Western NATO nations and the Soviet Union, a development which has had far-reaching, and perhaps damaging consequences for the alliance.

The military strategy of NATO also has not adjusted to the new circumstances that developed during the 1970s, relying still on an American long-range nuclear missile guarantee and on a disproportionate American share of the military burden. As we have seen, the future of the Western alliance clearly depends on the resolution of these three main issues which divide NATO nations today: strategic parity; conflicting views of détente and Soviet intentions; economic rivalry; and East-West trade.

Resolving these major problems may require a complete reassessment of the United States' dominant involvement in NATO and also of NATO's relationship to vital areas that lie outside of the original treaty regions of Western Europe and North America. Indeed, the Western alliance has never been an alliance among equal powers. The United States, NATO's only superpower, has always had special global interests and special obligations and duties within and without the alliance. But, in light of Europe's complete economic recovery from World War II, one foreign policy critic has suggested that it is time to end the extensive American protection of Western Europe. For their part, European NATO members frequently complain that they are asked by the United States to relinquish their political identities as sovereign nations and their right to decide where and when their military forces should be deployed. Many American policy analysts point to the serious issue of burden sharing—European reluctance to pay for Europe's defense. European NATO nations, many officials feel, should have an equal voice in alliance affairs, but they should first share the financial burden of NATO's military defense systems. In 1984, the Reagan Administration will spend roughly $240 billion on defense while all of the other European NATO members, with the exception of Great Britain, will spend a total of less than half of the American military budget.

Diverting dollars away from the civilian sector unavoidably hurts a country's economy and ultimately its standard of living. The Reagan Administration may be placing too much emphasis on military power and on the ability of military power to achieve diplomatic goals. Nonetheless, West European allies have shown no willingness to strengthen their neglected conventional ground forces, a move that would enable NATO to defend territories against limited military challenges in ways that nuclear weapons cannot. Most importantly, larger and better-equipped ground forces would vastly reduce the immediate risks of American nuclear intervention. Cost is one determining factor in the European reluctance to "share the burden," but Europeans also worry that very strong conventional military capabilities will weaken the nuclear guarantee link—the threat of using American nuclear forces to defend Europe—between the United States and Western Europe. Europeans want the American nuclear guarantee—through long-range ballistic missiles located in the United States, but not through nuclear missiles located on their own soil. The widespread European opposition to the deployment of the Pershing II missiles, which they originally requested, is an example of this double standard. Such attitudes of wanting to be defended by the United States but of not wanting to be associated with the American defense policies has created strong disenchantment with Europe in much of the United States Congress. As far back as 1973, a resolution to remove the 310,000 American troops from Western Europe was introduced and defeated in the U.S. Senate. Today there are 350,000 American soldiers in Europe with an equal number of dependents. In late 1982, a Senate Subcommittee on Defense voted to cut American troop involvement in Europe by 23,000 soldiers. Analysts believe that this measure may pass Congress because of some European nations' refusal to be more responsible and willing for their own protection.

The American troops in Europe, most of which are in West Germany, are a symbol of United States readiness and commitment to defend Western Europe, and troop reductions could depend on the future actions of the NATO allies, West Germany in particular.

United States forces in Germany hold maneuvers
in West Berlin with troops from other NATO countries,
to test a plan for the city's defense.

In contrast, some foreign policy critics point out that the United States may not want its NATO allies to decrease their reliance on American nuclear forces because this reliance gives the United States political leverage over the European nations. In any case, if the United States expects Western Europe to share equally the military costs of NATO's defense, it must also accept the equal partnership of its European allies.

NEW FRONTIERS

Another, and perhaps one of the most significant divisions among NATO members involves the need for NATO forces outside of the Atlantic Alliance's original boundaries. Article 6 of the NATO treaty established the Tropic of Cancer—which runs through Saudi Arabia—as the southernmost boundary of NATO's defense efforts. The United States has a global role along with, to a lesser extent, France and Great Britain in the defense of the Middle Eastern oil fields, or sea traffic routes which are vital to NATO. All other European NATO members, and particularly West Germany, maintain a strictly regional view of NATO's defense needs, looking only to central and northern Europe as essential defense zones.

American, French, and British perceptions of the Soviet threat, while not always harmonious, derive from a series of critical events that occurred throughout the 1970s and early 1980s: the first energy crisis in 1973–4, the direct Soviet and Cuban military intervention in Africa—in Angola in 1977, and in Ethiopia and Somalia in 1978—the Soviet invasion of Afghanistan in 1979, the Soviet crackdown in Poland in 1981, and the Soviet shooting down of a Korean commercial passenger jet in the Western Pacific in 1983. These events made it clear that the Soviets would resort to force, and not diplomacy, whenever it was necessary.

More importantly, the pattern of Soviet expansion of their sphere of influence focused on two geographical areas vital to NATO and the West—the Persian Gulf and southern Africa. Over 65 percent of Western Europe's and Japan's total oil needs and 100 percent of the daily needs of the American forces in Europe come from the nations surrounding the Persian Gulf. The Europe-bound oil tankers must pass through the narrow Strait of Hormuz, the "oil jugular" of the West. If a hostile military force were to control and blockade this narrow channel, it could quickly strangle the Western world.

Soviet military moves into Ethiopia, Yemen, and Afghanistan, all states which are very near to the Persian Gulf, along with the construction of a large Soviet forward airbase in southern Afghanistan that's only 200 miles from the Strait of Hormuz, have placed great importance on NATO's security responsibilities outside of the Tropic of Cancer. There is no area outside of the Soviet Union as important to the Soviets as the Persian Gulf is to NATO. The United States has taken the responsibility, along with the aid of France and Great Britain, of protecting and safeguarding the free flow of oil traffic in the Persian Gulf. The largest and most prosperous European NATO member, West Germany, consistently disassociates itself from any American, French, or British attempts at peacekeeping in the Middle East, in particular in 1983-84 in Beirut.

Another area outside of NATO's treaty boundaries which has been the location of much recent Soviet-aligned activity is Africa. By 1983, the Soviets had placed a total of 36,000 Cuban troops in Angola to support the Soviet-installed Communist government, along with thousands of Soviet military advisors in such African countries as Algeria, Namibia, Mozambique, and Libya. In the summer of 1983, Libya, a strongly pro-Soviet nation, invaded its southern neighbor, Chad, taking the first step in a Libyan strategy to militarily control a belt of Moslem countries across central Africa. Southern Africa, located below this Moslem belt, is vital to NATO because it is the West's main source of such strategic metals and minerals as chrome, titanium, platinum, gold, and diamonds which are used in the manufacture of many military weapons. In the summer of 1983, France rushed 3,000 soldiers and a squadron of jet fighters to Chad to halt the Libyan-backed invasion, while the United States provided $25 million in emergency military aid.

THE PITFALLS OF DÉTENTE

The significance of Persian Gulf oil, African strategic raw materials, and recent Soviet expansion has led to a current American expansion of its global military role. France and Britain have also shared some of the global role in NATO's security. West Germany and many other European nations, on the other hand, believe in and rely on détente—in the improvement of diplomatic and trade relations with the Soviet Union. To West Germany, détente is both stabilizing and beneficial and, as pointed out earlier, the only means for keeping their bridge to East Germany open. Détente also keeps the embers of their deep desires for reunification glowing, however futile such desires may be.

In chapters 6 and 7 we examined the "decoupling" effect, the detachment of the United States from Western Europe, which a decade of détente has already had in the NATO allies. When faced with the Afghanistan invasion and the Polish crackdown, the NATO alliance could not act within any political unity and was simply impotent. All NATO nations, especially West Germany, were conciliatory and paralyzed by their own commercial and political ties to Eastern Europe. Indeed, the economic damage done to the Soviet Union through selective American embargoes on grain supplies and pipeline equipment was vastly outweighed by the political damage, resulting from complete disagreement, done to NATO.

The response to the Soviet missile destruction of a Korean Airlines passenger jet which briefly and accidentally strayed into Soviet airspace in 1983 further illustrates the West's inability to act effectively against such an aggression. Although the Soviet act was in violation of all international flight agreements, NATO countries could not even agree to temporarily suspend air flights from the West to the Soviet Union.

There is a struggle going on for the future political orientation of Europe. West Germany is at the heart of the struggle. The United States would like to see the Germans and other NATO allies take much greater responsibility for their own defense, freeing American military for a larger global role. The struggle for Europe does not exist in the form of a sudden attack across the plains of central Europe or perhaps even in a threat to the Persian Gulf oil supplies. It exists in the long-term, Soviet objectives of dominating Western Europe, particularly West Germany, without firing a shot—through dependency on trade, on vital natural resources, and on diplomatic ties. When the Soviet's Siberian gas pipeline is completed in 1985, West Germany will double its dependence on Soviet gas. Such an energy dependence would enable the Soviets to exert major leverage by shutting down the supplies, in the event of a fabricated crisis, for the purpose of influencing German policies and actions.

Today the Soviets have targeted West Germany as their "go-between" or their window on the West. West Germany has become the direct "bridge" between East and West, relaying special messages from Moscow to Washington. In the 1960s, France, under Charles de Gaulle and later in 1980 under Valéry Giscard d'Estaing, was the bridge between East and West. Both de Gaulle and d'Estaing stayed in power through a tacit alliance with the French Communist Party. The Communists helped the Gaulists to squeeze out any effective opposition in return for foreign policy concessions and government post appointments. This was done with active Soviet support for the French Communist Party.

In just over a decade, the Soviet view of West Germany has come full circle. In 1970, the standard Soviet phrase for the West German capital, Bonn, was the "capital of Nazi revanchists," meaning that they were Nazis who wanted to reclaim their former lands. In 1983, it was reported that the Soviets were calling West Germany "a partner for peace." Flora Lewis, the foreign affairs correspondent of the New York Times, has written that, "The cold war began with the dispute over Germany, and its partition remains the dividing line of Europe." Undoubtedly, the Soviet dream is to achieve a neutralized West Germany and a politically isolated United States.

Neutralist nations in Europe needed only to look at the 1981 and 1982 Soviet submarine violations of Sweden's territorial waters to confirm the double-sided purpose of Soviet détente policies. The Soviets had for some time been proposing a nuclear-free Nordic zone. Their characteristic facade of cooperation and peacefulness was summarily unmasked, however, when nuclear-armed torpedoes were detected on the submarines, one of which went aground.

Security for the Western alliance is based on economic and political solidarity—on agreement over important issues, on shared economic institutions, and on common economic policies toward East-West trade—as much as it is on military strength. Agreement on issues, of course, is not necessary on all occasions. But it is essential in times of crisis. NATO is an alliance of free, independent nations, and diversity of opinion is the hallmark of this democratic association. While inter-alliance conflict and disagreement are as old as NATO itself, whether the Atlantic Alliance can withstand its current, long-term divisions is uncertain.

If NATO is to continue to exist and be effective, a new Atlanticism, or a new spirit of Atlantic cooperation, of understanding of each other's needs, and of shared responsibility between both the United States and Western Europe will be required. Whether or not this new Atlanticism is possible or even desirable is a question that remains unanswered.

Some foreign policy analysts write with complete assurance that NATO will continue to exist in the future because the United States and Western Europe have been allies for almost forty years. Anything is possible. As trade with Japan, China, Korea, Hong Kong, and Singapore becomes increasingly important to the United States, it may focus more and more of its military-security resources on that region of the Western Pacific, leaving Western Europe to accept most of the responsibility for its own defense.

The future of NATO and the future of American participation in the alliance lies in whether or not the conflicting views of détente can be resolved and whether or not West Germany and other European nations increase their share of the military costs of NATO. Finally, and perhaps most importantly, NATO's effectiveness depends on whether or not the other NATO members agree to join the United States, France, and Great Britain in providing a more ambitious framework for safeguarding Western security and protecting Western interests beyond the Tropic of Cancer.

FURTHER READING

NATO is a subject that is usually discussed within larger areas of concern: East-West military strategies, political relations between the United States and Europe, and post-war military history. There is very little literature specifically about NATO. A good, brief but somewhat outdated book which offers some detail about the operations and command structure of NATO is James R. Huntley's, *The NATO Story*, Manhattan Publishing Company, New York, 1969.

NATO publishes its own monthly newsletter, *The NATO Letter*, which keeps readers abreast of current NATO news and issues. It is probably available only at large or specialized libraries. The two most widely read quarterlies on foreign affairs, *Foreign Affairs* and *Foreign Policy* contain a great many articles on NATO in their issues. Both are highly informative if slightly different publications, and they should not be beyond the understanding of the diligent young adult reader.

For those interested in the details of NATO's military strength—numbers of troops, tanks, fighter planes, and ships—*The Military Balance*, published annually by the International Institute of Strategic Studies, is the undisputed last word on such matters. Readers who want to familiarize themselves with the background to the creation of NATO, specifically World War II, would do well to read the excellent and relatively brief, *History of the Second World War*, by B.H. Liddell-Hart, Putnam, New York, 1980. Finally, an interesting and informative sample of the genre of studies produced by defense "think tanks" is *The Soviet Threat to NATO's Northern Flank*, by Marian K. Leighton, National Strategy Information Center, Inc., New York, 1979. This book is not difficult, and it gives the reader a closer look at the military strategy problems confronting NATO.

INDEX

Finland, 5, 11, 73
Flexible response, 48–49
France, 15, 17, 21
  Algerian indepen-
    dence, 35, 37
  détente with Soviet
    Union, 54–55
  Suez Affair, 32, 34
  World War II, 4, 7

Germany:
  Postwar division of,
    10, 17, 18
  World War II, 4–5, 7–
    8
  See also East Germa-
    ny; West Germany
Great Britain, 21
  postwar policy, 8–12
  Suez Affair, 32, 34
  World War II, 4–5, 7
Greece, 11, 14, 21, 28, 38
Gross National Products
  (GNP), 62

Ho Chi Minh, 36
Hormuz, Strait of, 81
Hungary, 15, 17, 34–35

I.C.B.M.'s (Intercontinental
  Ballistic Missiles), 43–45
Indonesia, 29, 30 illus.
Iran, 11, 14
Italy, 15, 21

Japan, 4, 7
Johnson, Lyndon, 54

Kennan, George, 14
Kennedy, John F., 43, 53, 54

Khruschev, Nikita S., 53
Korea, 14. See also North
  Korea; South Korea

Lebanon, 37
Luxembourg, 17, 21

MacArthur, Douglas, 29
Mao-Tse-tung, 29
Marshall, George, 15, 18
Marshall Plan, 15–16, 25,
  38, 62
Middle East, 1, 11, 80–81
Mitterand, Francois, 47,
  55
Morocco, 35

Nasser, Gamel Abdel, 32
NATO:
  agencies of, 24–25
  articles of, 21–22
  burden sharing, 63,
    65–67, 77–78
  East–West détente,
    52–59
  East–West trade, 67–
    73
  first twenty years, 28–38
  strategic parity, 41–50
Netherlands, 21, 29
North Atlantic Treaty Or-
  ganization. See NATO
North Korea, 29, 31
Nuclear weapons, 40–50

Organization for Economic
  Cooperation and Devel-
  opment (OECD), 25

Palestine, 29